OLÉ! CINCO DE MAYO!

BY MARGARET MCMANIS
ILLUSTRATED BY DAVID HARRINGTON

PELICAN PUBLISHING COMPANY
GRETNA 2013

For two great kids, Jackson and Riley—D. H.

*The word "Pelican" and the depiction of a pelican are
trademarks of Pelican Publishing Company, Inc., and are
registered in the U.S. Patent and Trademark Office.*

Library of Congress Cataloging-in-Publication Data

McManis, Margaret Olivia.
  Olé! Cinco de Mayo! / Margaret McManis ; illustrated by David Harrington.
      p. cm.
  Summary: Using the rhythm of the round song, "Bingo," follows Pablo as
he brings a calf named Rodeo to school for its Cinco de Mayo festivities.
Includes glossary of Spanish words.
      ISBN 978-1-4556-1754-8 (hardcover : alk. paper) — ISBN 978-
1-4556-1755-5 (e-book) [1. Stories in rhyme. 2. Cows—Fiction. 3.
Animals—Infancy—Fiction. 4. Schools—Fiction. 5. Cinco de Mayo (Mexican
holiday)—Fiction. 6. Hispanic Americans—Fiction.] I. Harrington, David,
ill. II. Title.
  PZ8.3.M45988Olé 2013
  [E]—dc23

                              2012025142

Printed in Malaysia
Published by Pelican Publishing Company, Inc.
1000 Burmaster Street, Gretna, Louisiana 70053

OLÉ! CINCO DE MAYO!

Pablo has a little calf.
Rodeo is his name-o.
He brings the calf to school one day.
It is Cinco de Mayo.

He makes the *niños* laugh and play
Until the teacher shouts-o.
"He'll eat *mis libros* and *mi gis*.
Adios to you, Rodeo!"

CINCO

HISTORY

GEOGRAPHY

Pablo heads to PE class,
So very *ansioso*.
The ropes, the nets, they're quite a mess
Because of the *bandido*.

R-O-D-E-O, R-O-D-E-O, R-O-D-E-O,
Rodeo is his name-o.

The smell of *heno* so close by
Inside the *LMC-o*—
A book boss who is not amused,
Hotter than *habanero*.

"¡Ay caramba!" Tasty flan
So lovely and so yellow
Brings mouthfuls of sheer delight
To the spotted little fellow.

How he loves the school cafe.
He's ready to *comer*-o.
But the cafe cook is quite steamed up
Just like a *jalapeño!*

The art class next comes in his sights.
This is a special *día*.
Cinco de Mayo, the fifth of May—
Freedom brings us *alegría*.

The wall is hung with pictures bright,
Cow, horse, and armadillo,
But ribbons they taste mighty nice,
So flashy, full of *brillo*.

A pot of beans, a *rancho* scene,
Sits on the rustic stage-o;
Trough of *agua* nice and cold,
A playground for Rodeo.

Their principal in *vaquero* wear
Hands out *certificados*.
The red *serape* like a flag
Makes him quite *enojado*.

Kersplish, kersplash, a soggy bath!
No time for him to stay-o.
The principal with loud voice blasts,
"Hey, stop that wild *ternero!*"

"*¡Qué horror!*" Pablo cries in shock.
"What am I to do-o?
¡Ay caramba, oh my gosh,
He'll ruin Cinco de Mayo!"

Strumming from the music wing
Brings around Rodeo,
Scootin' down the winding hall,
Ears pricked and all akimbo.

Waiting for the coming crash,
The *niños* are concerned-o—
Pablo most of all, wide eyed
And very *nervioso*.

But guitar strings and square-dance chords
Have calmed our little beast-o.
Pablo smiles and laughs aloud.
"Can that calf do-si-do-o!"

The conga line flows down the hall
With Pablo quick to follow.
He throws a *beso*; all join in:
"¡*Olé*, Cinco de Mayo!"

GLOSSARY

agua (AH-gwah)—water

alegría (ah-leh-GREE-ah)—happiness

ansioso (ahn-see-O-so)—anxious

ay caramba (eye cah-ROM-bah)—oh my gosh

bandido (ban-DEE-doh)—bandit

beso (BEH-so)—kiss

book boss—librarian

brillo (BREE-o)—shine

certificados (sehr-tee-fee-CAH-doz)—certificates

comer (co-MAIR)—eat

día (DEE-ah)—day

enojado (en-o-HAH-doh)—mad

flan (flahn)—custard

habanero (hah-bah-NAIR-o)—a fiery hot pepper similar to the Scotch bonnet

heno (HAY-no)—hay

jalapeño (hah-la-PAYN-yo)—a hot pepper

LMC— library media center

mi gis (mee geess)—my chalk

mis libros (meess LEE-brohss)—my books

nervioso (nuhr-vee-O-so)—nervous

niños (NEEN-yohss)—children

olé (o-LAY)—bravo

qué horror (kay hohr-ROHR)—what a horror

rancho (RON-cho)—ranch

Rodeo (Ro-DAY-o)—rodeo

serape (sehr-AH-pay)—shawl

ternero (tehr-NAIR-o)—calf

vaquero (vah-KAIR-o)—cowboy

EASY FLAN RECIPE

Butter to grease pan
Flour for pan
1¼ cups flour
⅔ cup sugar
Pinch of salt
4 eggs
4 cups milk
1 tsp. vanilla extract

Before you start, get a grownup to help preheat the oven to 425 degrees.
Grease and flour a 9-inch-square baking pan.

Step 1. Measure 1¼ cups flour into a large mixing bowl.
Step 2. Form a hole in the center of the flour, and pour in the sugar and salt.
Step 3. In another bowl, beat the eggs with a whisk or fork.
Step 4. Add the eggs to the center of the flour mixture.
Step 5. Pour in the milk slowly, stirring as you go. Continue stirring until you have a smooth batter.
Step 6. Stir in the vanilla.
Step 7. Pour the batter into the baking pan.
Step 8. Bake at 425 degrees for 45 minutes.
Step 9. Let cool completely and refrigerate for at least 4 hours before serving.

SONG

Pablo has a little calf.
Rodeo is his name-o.
R-O-D-E-O,
R-O-D-E-O,
R-O-D-E-O,
Rodeo is his name-o.
Pablo has a little calf.
Rodeo is his name-o.
(Clap) *O-D-E-O*,
(Clap) *O-D-E-O*,
(Clap) *O-D-E-O*,
Rodeo is his name-o.
Pablo has a little calf.
Rodeo is his name-o.
(Clap-clap) *D-E-O*,
(Clap-clap) *D-E-O*,
(Clap-clap) *D-E-O*,
Rodeo is his name-o.

Pablo has a little calf.
Rodeo is his name-o.
(Clap-clap-clap) *E-O*,
(Clap-clap-clap) *E-O*,
(Clap-clap-clap) *E-O*,
Rodeo is his name-o.
Pablo has a little calf.
Rodeo is his name-o.
(Clap-clap-clap-clap) *O*,
(Clap-clap-clap-clap) *O*,
(Clap-clap-clap-clap) *O*,
Rodeo is his name-o.
Pablo has a little calf.
Rodeo is his name-o.
(Clap-clap-clap-clap-clap),
(Clap-clap-clap-clap-clap),
(Clap-clap-clap-clap-clap),
And Rodeo is his name-o.

CINCO DE MAYO HISTORY

Cinco de Mayo—or the fifth of May—is a holiday celebrating the Mexican army's 1862 victory over the French at the Battle of Puebla during the Franco-Mexican War (1861-67). The French sent 8,000 troops against 4,000 Mexicans, and the battle lasted from daybreak until early evening. The French lost around 500 men, while the Mexicans lost only 100 men. The French finally retreated.

Gen. Ignacio Zaragoza Seguín became the hero of the day, and the date of the successful battle evolved into a celebration of Mexican culture and heritage. Today it is marked in the U.S. in states that have a large Hispanic population. Festivities include parades, school celebrations, mariachi music, folk-dancing performances, and enjoying traditional foods such as tacos and flan.